Vegan: I am vegan

Vegan Cookbook recipes for Yoga Lovers

by

Sammy Hermans

Copyright

Copyright © 2016 by Sammy Hermans. All rights reserved. All registered trademarks in this book are property of their respective owners. Nothing of this book may be reproduced or transmitted in any form or by any means: electronic, mechanical, recording, photographing, photocopying, reprinted or otherwise; without the written permission of the author Sammy Hermans.

The information in this book has been provided for educational and entertainment purposes only. Respective authors own all copyrights that are not in the possession of the publisher.

The information contained in this book has been compiled from sources deemed reliable and it is accurate to the author's best knowledge, however the author can not guarantee the accuracy and validity and can not be held liable for any errors or omissions.

By using the knowledge in this book you agree to hold harmless the author, from and against any damages, costs and expenses, including any legal fees. You agree to accept all risks of using the information in this book.

Contents

Copyright..1
How will this book benefit YOU?...3
Thank You..4
The author 5
Introduction 6
Chapter 1: Grow Your Food Intelligence 7
Chapter 2: Why Vegan?...8
Chapter 3: The Vegan cookbook..10
Thanks and Credits...60
A helping hand for the author..61
Extra Bonus..63
Chapter 1: Can the 10 DAYS program really work for me?................63

How will this book benefit YOU?

You will:

- Understand why you need to eat Yoga vegan food,
- Learn how Yoga vegan food will benefit your health,
- Find out how Yoga vegan food will give you more energy
- Get encouraged to change your life in a positive Vegan way,
- Feel better after reading this book,
- Digest food better;
- Start learning what to do to feel better all day,
- Know what road to take to become happier,
- Cook cheaper but healthier,
- Have more confidence when you finished this book to start with Yoga vegan food,
- Make a switch to your lifestyle in a positive direction,
- Accomplish a new way of thinking,
- Motivate yourself to become a better person,
- Convince other family members to start with Yoga vegan food,
- Have fun by reading this easy to read Vegan book,
- Understand why Yoga vegan food can change your life Today in the healthy way.

Thank You

I would like to begin this book by thanking you to read one of the books I have written to change your life. I know your time is valuable and I am very grateful that you decided to take a little time out of your day to read my book. I am sure you will be happy after reading this Vegan cookbook.

Thank You and enjoy.

The author

Sammy Hermans is an upcoming author that was born in the early 80's and has since childhood a great interest in the Yoga art. He was studying multiple Yoga styles and grew up in Belgium, the capital of Europe. The author is a real world citizen and likes to get new influences from all over the world.

The author loves to do research about the different Yoga styles to implement them in the Yoga classes and help people to find the best Yoga styles that fits them. Meditation has helped him gain control over his mind and live a stress-free, more productive, healthy and happier life. Sammy enjoys seeing the wonderful improvements in peoples lives through yoga. He loves to help people with this new lifestyle and guide them through this healthy journey. The author is always willing to help people to become happier and healthier.

The author started a Yoga training and Yoga coaching business together with his partner Sherley Henry De Hermans. The company 'Yoga Latinos' was created to help people along their journey towards a healthy Yoga life. Together they are willing to help and guide everybody in their new mindset.

Sammy's other interests include world music, dancing, relaxing and meditation, multimedia arts, reading, traveling, spending time in nature & drinking cups of tea and enjoying time with his wife, kids and family.

Discover all the amazing ideas in his books.

Introduction

Thank you for purchasing this Vegan cookbook. This is a book about how to adopt and enjoy a long-term vegan lifestyle. Maybe you want to become a real Yogi it is important to understand that you are what you eat. By eating vegan you will be more aware of yourself and your environment. Let's start by including advice on transitioning. I will provide you with 25 delicious vegan recipes with tasty pictures.

Get started with eating vegan food and turn your favorite non-vegan foods into vegan ones by making simple adjustments. This isn't necessarily the healthiest way to go vegan, but it's a convenient way to get the animal ingredients out of your diet and it will be much easier to maintain. Once you've been eating vegan for a while, you can make further improvements from there. Eating vegan will help you with having more energy to start with your Yoga exercises.

Finding vegan replacements for your favorite foods will motivate you to continue the Vegan lifestyle. Learn to eat a veggie burger instead of a cow burger. Ice cream becomes soy ice cream or coconut ice cream, and so on. Preparing Vegan recipes is easy. If there's any food you're craving to make vegan, someone has probably already shared a quality recipe for it. Find out the vegan recipes in this book and enjoy.

Chapter 1: Grow Your Food Intelligence

Being a vegan you can expect to increase your food intelligence greatly. When you learn the truth about what you used to eat, you will probably feel sorry for the people who are still being duped. If you still want to buy prepackaged foods, get used to reading nutrition labels. Get used to scanning for animal ingredients on the food labels. As soon as you identify a single animal ingredient such as milk powder or whey, you can put the package down.

Some vegans prefer not to eat packaged foods at all. This is a personal choice. The food industry certainly sells some incredibly bad products that will damage your health in the long run. But I wouldn't say all the players are bad. It's okay with buying some packaged foods, but better avoid the major mainstream American brands.

Also, be on the lookout for bogus, healthy-sounding words on food packages like whole or natural, which are largely meaningless. Organic (or Bio in Europe) is a word that actually has legal meaning. When you see legally meaningless terms that are obviously trying to make a product sound healthy, you can usually assume that the product is as phony as it's labeling. The products that look like they're trying too hard to appear healthy are usually unhealthy.

As a quick shortcut, look at the cholesterol line on the nutrition label. If you see anything other than zero mg cholesterol, the food isn't vegan, since plant-based foods never contain any cholesterol. Cholesterol only comes from animal ingredients. But if the cholesterol is zero, you'll still need to check the ingredients since there may still be small amounts of animal ingredients. If you see an ingredient you don't recognize, feel free to Google it. Gradually educate yourself on what each ingredient is. If you can't figure it out, maybe you shouldn't be eating it anyway.

Chapter 2: Why Vegan?

Buy organic food whenever possible

Buy organic food whenever possible, but if you are more sensitive to price, I wouldn't worry about pesticides too much. As a vegan you will still be ingesting fewer pesticides than animal eaters, since pesticides accumulate in animal tissues.

Generally it's better to buy food from Whole Foods, Costco, Trader Joe's or from local farmers markets. Costco sells organic mixed greens, spinach, carrots, sweet potatoes, bananas, blueberries, soy milk, rice, pasta, udon noodles, hummus, frozen berries, and lots of other organic items too.

Another benefit from this shop is that Costco pays their employees well, so I see the same people working there year after year; they have virtually no employee turnover. Walmart, by comparison, it seems just downright bad, especially in how they treat their employees.

You should avoid shopping there. For many vegans it doesn't feel good to support a company that also sells animal products, even if we aren't buying any of those products directly. You will have to discover yourself how much of a purist you want to be. As more people go vegan, new possibilities will become viable. For now, do the best you can with what's available in your area.

Eat Vegan for little money

Eating vegan can be very inexpensive if you want it to be. Rice, beans, pasta, potatoes, sweet potatoes, oats, bananas, millet, quinoa, and many other foods can provide plenty of calories at low cost. You can live quite comfortably off low-cost foods, which have been the basis of large modern civilizations for millenniums.

Vegan is easy to prepare

The same goes for eating vegan on a time budget. How long does it take to eat some fruit? When you are in a hurry, you can make a meal out of several bananas. Apples are easy to eat while driving. Rice takes a while to cook, but very little active preparation time.

If someone complains to me about the financial cost or the time cost of eating vegan, I'd try to figure out if they're ignorant, lazy, or just don't understand. In my experience, it's frequently a blend of all three: ignorance and laziness and general misunderstanding. Fortunately, those are all treatable conditions for those who wish to be cured.

You can be sure, eating vegan is also a lot less burdensome on the environment and on our resources like water, electricity, and fuel. Instead of growing plant foods, feeding them to animals, and then eating the animals, it's much more efficient all around to eat plant foods directly.

Chapter 3: The Vegan cookbook

1) Almond Milk Oats with Chia Seeds

Ingredients:

2 bananas (mashed)
1 cup rolled oats
1 1/2 cup almond milk
1 cup rolled oats
1/2 tsp cinnamon
4 tbsp. chia seeds
8 strawberries (diced)
20 blueberries

Preparations and cooking:
Place the sliced bananas in a small bowl and mash them with a fork until there are no big chunks anymore. Add the chia seeds and the cinnamon, then blend together.

You can add the strawberries and blueberries to make it more tasty. Stir in the oats and almond milk. Refrigerate overnight for the best flavor value.

Persons:
2 persons

Duration:
5-10 minutes or overnight

2) Granola

Ingredients:

4 cups rolled oats
1 cup almonds, chopped
1 cup uncooked millet
1 tsp cinnamon
4 tbsp. ground flax
4 vanilla beans, scraped
2 tbsp. chia seeds
6 strawberries
1/2 cup Brown sugar
1 tsp kosher salt, or to taste
4 tbsp. applesauce
1/2 cup Brown Rice Syrup
6 tbsp. Almond Butter
2 tsp pure vanilla extract
1 tsp almond extract

Preparations and cooking:
Preheat the oven at 150 degrees (300F). Mix wet and dry the ingredients in separate bowls. Wet ingredients for 60 seconds in the microwave.

Stir until a smooth texture is achieved. Pour the wet mixture in dry ingredients and blend well. Cool for at least 15 minutes, then serve.

Persons:
2 persons

Duration:
20-25 minutes

3) Meatless Moussaka

Ingredients:

6 cups dry brown or yellow lentils
2 giant potatoes rinsed and drained
1 cup water
1 stalk celery, diced tremendous
1 medium sweet onion, peeled and diced
3 cloves garlic, minced
½ tsp salt
¼ tsp ground cinnamon
¼ freshly ground black pepper
¼ tsp dried basil
¼ tsp dried oregano
¼ tsp dried parsley
1 medium eggplant, diced
12 baby carrots, cut into three items
2 cups Roma tomatoes, diced
1 (eight-ounce) bundle vegan cream cheese, softened

Preparations and cooking:

Put the lentils, potatoes, water, celery, onion, garlic, salt, cinnamon, pepper, basil, oregano, and parsley to a four-quart slow cooker. Stir everything.

Top with eggplant and carrots. In case you get your eggplant in the grocery store and suspect that it's been waxed, peel it earlier than dicing it and including it to the slow cooker. Cover and cook on low for six hours, or untill the lentils are cooked. Stir within the tomatoes and add a dollop of vegan cream cheese over the lentil combination. Cover and cook on low for an extra ½ hour.

Persons:

4 persons

Duration:

7-8 hours

4) Creamy Mushroom Soup

Ingredients:

1 ½ cup whole button mushrooms ½ cup baby bellas (sliced)
2 garlic cloves
3 cups vegetable broth
1 ¼ cup almond milk
1/ 8 tsp. white pepper
2 shallots Kosher salt to taste
4 tbsp olive oil

Preparations and cooking:

Preheat oven to 230 degrees (450F). After place the mushrooms on a baking sheet and sprinkle with olive oil and salt. Cook for 20 minutes. Sauté the shallots for 2 minutes and add in baby bellas. When the bellas are golden brown, add in the garlic and sherry. Now cook until the mixture is reduced to its half.

Add in the vegetable broth and simmer for 10-15 minutes. Add mushrooms in the soup and use a food processor to blend until smooth. Pour the mixture back into a saucepan and add in pepper and almond milk. Let it simmer for 3-5 minutes before serving.

Persons:

2 persons

Duration:

40-45 minutes

5) Avocado Pasta

Ingredients:

12 oz. spaghetti
2 ripe avocados, halved, seeded and peeled
½ cup fresh basil leaves
2 cloves garlic
2 tbsp. lemon juice
Kosher salt and freshly ground black pepper to taste
1/ 3 cup olive oil
1 cup cherry tomatoes
½ cup canned corn kernels

Preparations and cooking:

Cook the pasta according to the detailed instruction; drain and apply a bit of oil to keep pasta from sticking to each other. Blend the avocado, lemon juice, olive oil, basil and garlic using a food processor.

Make sure that the sauce is smooth with no avocado chunks. Mix the pasta with the avocado sauce in a bowl, and add the cherry tomatoes and corn before diving in.

Persons:

2 persons

Duration:

20-25 minutes

6) Rice Noodles with Tofu

Ingredients:

3 oz. package rice noodles
1/2 cup brown sugar
1/2 cup soya sauce
4 tbsp. fresh lime juice
2 oz. package firm tofu, cut
2 tbsp. canola oil
4 carrots, cut
2 red bell pepper, sliced
2 tbsp. grated fresh ginger
4 cups bean sprouts
8 scallions, sliced
1/2 cup roasted peanuts, chopped
1 cup fresh cilantro

Preparations and cooking:

Cook noodles according to detailed instructions, drain and set aside. Mix sugar, lime juice and soya sauce in a small bowl. Remove any excess liquid from tofu slices and cut them into ½ inch pieces. Cook carrots, bell pepper and ginger for 2 minutes, stirring frequently.

Add in bean sprouts and tofu, and cook for an additional 3-4 minutes. When vegetables are slightly tender, add noodles in with half of the soya sauce mix. Cook for 2 minutes before transferring your noodles on a plate and topping them with the remaining soya sauce mix. Sprinkle with peanuts or cilantro, if desired.

Persons:

4 persons

Duration:

15-20 minutes

7) Piña Colada

Ingredients:

1 can (20 oz.) crushed pineapple in juice
1 can (13.5 oz.) coconut milk
3 bananas, peeled and frozen
2 slices of pineapple
¼ cup shredded coconut

Preparations and cooking:

Mix the pineapple, coconut milk and bananas in a food processor untill blended smooth. Garnish with a slice of pineapple and spread some shredded coconut around and on top.

Persons:

2 persons

Duration:

5-10 minutes

8) Banana Bread

Ingredients:

1 tsp apple cider vinegar
1 cup whole wheat flour
3 cups flour
2 tsp vanilla
2 cups vegan butter
2 cups brown sugar
6 mashed bananas
2 tsp baking powder
2 tsp baking soda
1/2 tsp nutmeg
1/2 tsp salt
1 1/2 cup toasted and chopped walnuts

Preparations and cooking:

Preheat the oven to 175 degrees (350F). Grease and flour a 9" loaf pan. After add vinegar to the vegan milk in a small bowl and stir Mix the vegan butter and sugar in a large bowl.

Add the milk mixture, along with the bananas and vanilla to the large bowl and mix well. Mix together flours, baking soda, baking powder, nutmeg, and salt in another bowl Add the mixture to the large bowl and beat well. Now you can add the walnuts.

Pour mixture into pan and bake for about 45 minutes. Check if the bread is done by inserting a toothpick near the center of the loaf. If it comes out mostly clean then the loaf is done. Cool for ten minutes on the pan, then place on a dish and let it cool fully.

Persons:

6 persons

Duration:

55-60 minutes

9) Coconut Macaroon

Ingredients:

1 1/2 cup all-purpose flour
6 cups unsweetened shredded coconut
2 cups sugar
1 cup non-dairy milk
4 tbsp. brown rice syrup
2 tsp salt
4 tsp vanilla extract
12 strawberries

Preparations and cooking:

Preheat the oven to 175 degrees (350F). Mix the sugar, milk, brown rice syrup, vanilla extract, and salt in a mixing bowl. Now add the flour to a mixing bowl and mix well. Dough should be thick enough to need mixing by hand.

Form small balls from the mixture and place on a lightly oiled cookie sheet. Shape balls as wished. Bake for ten minutes. Switch the baking sheets on the racks at around the 5-minute mark. Take the macaroons out of the oven and let them cool down. Macaroon tastes great with strawberries aside.

Persons:

4 persons

Duration:

20-25 minutes

10) Strawberry cheesecake

Ingredients:

Crust:
1 cup buckwheat flour
8 medjool dates
1/2 cup walnuts
1/4 tsp salt
1/2 tsp vanilla extract

Filling:
1 cup coconut milk
1/4 cup coconut oil
2 cups soaked cashews
4 medjool dates
1/4 tsp salt Juice of 1 lemon
2 tsp vanilla extract

Strawberry frosting:
2 cups strawberries
4 Medjool dates Juice
1/2 lemon

Preparations and cooking:

Crust:
Blend the walnuts and buckwheat flour. Add the dates, salt and vanilla to the flour mixture and blend until the mixture begins to stick together. Press the dough into a 9 inch pan to make the crust.

Filling:
Combine all the ingredients, except coconut oil, into a blender. Melt the coconut oil and add into the mixture until its well combined. Pour the filling onto the crust and place it in the

refrigerator for about two hours.

Frosting:
Blend strawberries with the dates and lemon juice. When the filling on the cake is hard enough pour the strawberry frosting on top of it and garnish with fresh strawberries to serve.

Persons:

4 persons

Duration:

2 ½-3 hours

11) Watermelon Cake

Ingredients:

1 watermelon
1 cup soaked hemp seeds
1 cup soaked cashews
½ cup coconut water
1 juiced lemon
2 vanilla beans
3 tablespoons raw honey
½ cup soaked almonds

Preparations and cooking:

Start by peeling the watermelon and shaping it to your desired size of cake. Cup cakes are also possible. Next, blend or process the rest of the ingredients until smooth.

Cover the entire cups with watermelon. Process the almonds and stick them to the sides of your cake. Top with your favorite fruits and refrigerate for an hour!

Persons:

6 persons

Duration:

1 ½ -2 hours

12) Taco (Guacamole and Tomatoes)

Ingredients:

2 (14.5 oz.) can whole tomatoes, drained, rinsed, patted dry
4 roma tomatoes, quartered
2 onion, chopped, divided
2 clove garlic, coarsely chopped
1 fresh cilantro
2 jalapeno pepper
salt and pepper to taste
8 avocados, halved with pits removed
20 (6 inch) whole wheat tortillas
2 (15 oz.) can kidney beans, rinsed and drained
4 torn romaine lettuce

Preparations and cooking:

Set your oven to 175 degrees (350F) before starting. Enter the following into a blender or processor: Jalapenos, fresh and canned tomatoes, garlic, and half of your onions. Process or pulse a few times. Do not make a smooth mix.

Only dice the contents a bit. Get a bowl, mix until smooth: pepper, the rest of the onions, salt, and avocados. Get a casserole dish and cook your tortillas in the oven for 5 minutes. Layer on each tortilla: lettuce, guacamole, salsa, and beans.

Persons:

4 persons

Duration:

15-20 minutes

13) Taco (Pumpkin and Avocado)

Ingredients:

2 tbsps vegetable oil
2 cups cubed fresh pumpkin
1/2 cup vegetable stock
1 tbsp ground cumin
salt and ground black pepper to taste
12 flour or corn tortillas, warmed
3/4 cup diced fresh tomato
1/2 cup diced onion
1/2 cup diced ripe avocado
3 tbsps chopped fresh cilantro

Preparations and cooking:

Stir fry your pumpkin for 5 mins in hot oil. Then add in your pepper, salt, veggie stock and cumin. Cook for 10 mins. Layer the following on your tortillas: pumpkin mix, cilantro, tomato, onion, diced avocado.

Persons:

4 persons

Duration:

15-20 minutes

14) Kiwi Green Smoothie Yield:

Ingredients:

2 cups chopped kale leaves
2 cups chopped Romaine lettuce
2 cups chopped Swiss chard leaves 1 cup sliced ripe bananas
2 kiwi fruit
1 lemon
2 cups distilled water
2 teaspoons bee pollen
1 teaspoon maca powder

Preparations and cooking:

Replace the water with the same amount of unsweetened coconut water for extra alkaline in your green smoothie. Mix all ingredients together and blend until smooth. If kiwis are not in season, substitute it with mango or papaya.

By adding nutrition supplements like bee pollen and maca powder in your green smoothie, you will increase health benefits that your body acquire.

Persons:

2 persons

Duration:

5-10 minutes

15) Apple Broccoli Detox Smoothie

Ingredients:

2 cups shredded romaine lettuce
1 cup broccoli heads
2 medium sized apples
1 orange
1 cup distilled water
2 cups ice cubes

Preparations and cooking:

Rinse greens under running water. Peel and core the apples. Cut them into 1-inch cubes. Mix all ingredients together and blend until smooth. Add 1 tablespoon of chopped parsley into the mix for an added kick.

This smoothie recipe is full of fiber, minerals, vitamins and phytochemicals that will rid your digestive system of toxins. This smoothie will improve your mental clarity and brain functioning, and revitalize your body. A great drink for a good detox cure.

Persons :

2 persons

Duration:

5-10 minutes

16) Pineapple and Coconut Spinach Smoothie

Ingredients:

2 cups spinach
4 cups pineapple chunks
1/2 cup coconut milk
1 cup water
1 cup ice cubes

Preparations and cooking:

Place all ingredients in a blender. Blend until mixed good. Pour into a glass and serve immediately. This is a refreshing smoothie that packs in dietary fibers, antioxidants and vitamins A and C.

Persons:

2 persons

Duration:

5-10 minutes

17) Broccoli and Blueberry

Ingredients:

1 cup broccoli
1 cup blueberries
1 cup sliced bananas
1 cup oats
2 tablespoons sunflower seeds
1 cup non-dairy milk of your choice
1 cup water
1 cup ice cubes

Preparations and cooking:

Put the ice cubes, water and broccoli together. Add ¼ cup raisins (or any other dried fruit) for a more fiber packed smoothie. Blueberries are an excellent fruit for weight loss because they help getting rid of belly fat and they accelerate the reduction of overall body weight.

Broccoli is an excellent vegetable for losing weight because it is rich in foliate, manganese and vitamins A and K. It is also high in fiber and very low in cholesterol.

Persons:

2 persons

Duration:

5-10 minutes

18) Italian Tomato Sauce

Ingredients:

2 cans (28 ounces each) whole or diced fire-roasted tomatoes
6 tablespoons olive oil
2 cans (6 ounces each) tomato paste 2 green bell peppers, diced
2 large onions, diced
10 cloves garlic, minced
2 tablespoons honey
2 teaspoons salt or to taste
Freshly ground black pepper to taste
8 teaspoons Italian seasoning

Preparations and cooking:

Place a saucepan at medium heat. Add thf olive oil. When the oil is heated, add the onions and bell pepper, and sauté until translucent. Add the tomatoes, tomato paste, honey, salt and pepper. Lower the heat. Cover partially and simmer for about 30minutes. Add garlic and simmer for another 10 minutes.

Add parsley. Mix well, remove from heat, and cool completely. Transfer into an airtight container and refrigerate until use. This sauce can be used in kinds of pasta, pizzas, dips, etc.

Persons:

6 persons

Duration:

60 minutes

19) Spiced couscous salad with bell pepper and zucchine

Ingredients :

4 cups Vegetable Broth
4 cups couscous
2 teaspoons cumin
1 teaspoon turmeric
1 teaspoon paprika
1/2 teaspoon cayenne pepper
2 tablespoons lemon juice
4 zucchinis, sliced
2 red bell peppers, chopped
2 yellow bell peppers, chopped
6 cloves garlic, minced
4 tablespoons olive oil
4 tablespoons chopped fresh parsley
Salt and pepper to taste

Preparations and cooking:

Mix the Vegetable Broth and couscous and put to boil. Add cumin, turmeric, paprika, cayenne pepper, and stir to mix. Flip off heat, cover, and wait minimum quarter-hour, until the couscous is mushy and the liquid is absorbed.

Fluff couscous with a fork and add lemon juice. Sauté zucchinis, bell peppers, garlic in olive oil simply till tender; mix with couscous. Add parsley. Season evenly with salt and pepper.

Persons:

4 persons

Duration:

20-25 minutes

20) Vegan Pizza Rolls

Ingredients:

Pizza dough:
5 cups all-purpose flour
1 package active dry yeast (about 2 teaspoons)
1 teaspoon sugar
2 teaspoons sea salt
2 tablespoons olive oil
1 1/2 cup warm water

The rolls:
Marinara sauce as required
Basil pesto as required

Preparations and cooking:

Add warm water, yeast and sugar to a large bowl and set aside for a few minutes until the mixture becomes bubbly and frothy. Add flour, salt, and oil and knead to a soft dough. Place dough in a greased bowl. (You can grease it with olive oil) Set this aside for about an hour or until the dough rises.

Once the dough rises, knead it for a short period. Roll the dough into a rectangle of about 11 inches by 7 inches. Spread pesto all over the rolled dough. Spread marinara sauce over pesto. Roll the rectangle gently. Use a sharp knife to cut the roll into about 3-4 pieces. Place the chopped pieces on a lined baking sheet.

Give sufficient gaps between the pieces on the baking sheet. Place the baking sheet in a warm place for about 30-40 minutes. Place the baking sheet in a preheated oven and bake at 175 degrees (350F) for about 30 minutes or until golden brown. Remove from the oven and cool for a few minutes. Serve with marinara sauce.

Persons:

3-4 persons

Duration:

1 ½ - 2 hours

21) Vegetable Soup:

Ingredients:

4 cans (14.5 ounces each) vegetable broth
2 cans (15 ounces each) kidney beans, drained
2 cans (28 ounces each) peeled, crushed tomatoes
7 small zucchinis, chopped into cubes
1 cup frozen green beans
4 large carrots, chopped
5 cloves garlic, minced
1 cup frozen pearl onions
3 stalks celery, chopped into thick slices
3 bay leaves
1 teaspoon dried basil
2 tablespoons dried parsley
1 cup macaroni
2 cubes vegetable bouillon
Salt to taste
Pepper powder to taste

Preparations and cooking:

Place a large saucepan or pot at medium heat. Add broth, tomatoes, carrots, beans, celery, onions, garlic, parsley, basil, and bay leaf along with vegetable bouillon cubes and bring to boil. Add the rest of the ingredients and bring to boil.

Lower the heat and simmer until thr macaroni is al dente. Remove from heat and discard bay leaf. Serve.

Persons:

4-6 persons

Duration:

15-20 minutes

22) Pasta Salad:

Ingredients:

7 ounces fusilli pasta
2 small green bell peppers, chopped 2 medium onions, chopped
1 cup mushrooms, chopped
2 ripe tomatoes, chopped
1 cup feta cheese
8 tablespoons vegan fat-free Italian style dressing

Preparations and cooking:

Start with the fusilli pasta, cook according to instructions on package. Add all the ingredients except the dressing to a bowl and toss well. Pour dressing and toss again. Taste and add more dressing if necessary. Chill for about 10 minutes and serve.

Persons:

2 persons

Duration:

25-30 minutes

23) Vegan Meatballs

Ingredients:

1 medium yellow onion, chopped
2 cups mushrooms, chopped
1 tablespoon parsley, chopped
1 clove garlic, minced
½ tablespoon extra virgin olive oil ½ can (15 ounces) cannellini beans, rinsed, drained
½ jar (7 ounces) roasted peppers, drained
¼ cup seasoned bread crumbs
¼ teaspoon salt to taste
¼ teaspoon freshly ground pepper or to taste
Tomato sauce as required (refer to recipe Italian tomato sauce)
Whole wheat spaghetti to serve, cooked
2 tablespoons vegan cheese to serve
Cooking spray

Preparations and cooking:

Place a skillet over medium heat. Add olive oil. When oil is heated, add onions and sauté until the onions are soft. Add mushrooms and sauté until mushrooms are soft. Remove from heat and cool for a while. Transfer into a food processor bowl. Add beans and pepper, and pulse until the contents are chopped into smaller pieces. Put them into a bowl. Add breadcrumbs, salt, pepper and cheese. Mix well, cover and chill for an hour.

Grease the muffin tins with cooking spray. Drop about 2 tablespoons of the mixture into each of the muffin cavities. Bake in a preheated oven at 175 degrees (350F) for about 25 minutes. Remove from oven and cool for 5 minutes. Run a knife all around the edges of the meatballs and remove the meatballs. Add spaghetti to a skillet and place over high heat. Pour tomato sauce as required and toss well.

Persons:

4 persons

Duration:

35-40 minutes

24) Banana Ice:

Ingredients:

Juice of 6 lemons
Juice of 6 oranges
1 cup sugar
3 cups water
6 bananas, peeled, cut into small pieces
2 cans (8 ounces each) crushed pineapples
Lemon-lime soda (optional)
A few mint sprigs to garnish

Preparations and cooking:

Place a saucepan over medium heat. Add sugar and water and bring to boil. When sugar dissolves, remove from heat and let it cool completely. Pour into a freezable dish. Add orange and lemon juice, crushed pineapple and banana pieces. Mix everything well. Freeze until it's done. Remove from freezer about 5-10 minutes before serving.

Beat it mildly with a spoon. You should get a consistency of slush. Garnish with mint sprigs and serve. If you are using lemon-lime soda, then pour over the ice and serve.

Persons:

6-8 persons

Duration:

3-4 hours

25) Wild mushroom risotto

Ingredients:

1 teaspoon olive oil
1 shallot, minced
2 cloves garlic, minced
8 ounces sliced assorted wild mushrooms
2 cups arborio rice
2 cups Vegetable Broth
3 cups water
½ teaspoon salt

Preparations and cooking:

Heat the oil in a nonstick pan. Sauté the shallot, garlic and mushrooms till mushy, about 4–5 minutes. Add the rice and ½ cup Vegetable Broth and cook until the liquid is totally absorbed, about five minutes.

Scrape the rice combination right into a four-quart slow cooker. Add the water, salt and the remaining Vegetable Broth. Cover and cook on low heat for two hours. Stir earlier than serving.

Persons:

3-4 persons

Duration:

2 ½ hours

Thanks and Credits

Thanks to everybody that supported me with writing this Yoga book. Special thanks goes to my partner Sherley Henry De Hermans. She helped with research and advice to accomplish this Vegan cookbook.

Sherley Henry De Hermans is a Yoga teacher for the company Yoga Latinos and has several years experience with teaching different Yoga styles and knows different poses and techniques. However she mainly concentrates on Hatha Yoga, Vinyasa Yoga, Ashantha Yoga and Dance Yoga, but she is also an expert in massage and pressure point techniques.

If you are looking for professional help and a perfect guide during your Yoga journey, you can contact Sherley on www.yogalatinos.com for online Yoga classes.

Together we are a Yoga team and we are willing to help you with all your health problems or just getting you to the next Yoga level.

The attitude of gratitude is the highest Yoga.

A helping hand for the author

Thank you for purchasing this book and reading it. I hope you will be happy with this "Vegan cookbook for Yoga Lovers" and enjoyed it. You are now ready to start your journey throughout the Yoga world.

In order to make it possible to do more research and to write more books, it is important to get your full support. You can help a lot by putting some honest reviews on the Amazon Kindle book reviews section. Please keep in mind that by giving a honest five star rate, you will support the author.

If you like the "Vegan cookbook", and you want to read more Yoga related books, please check out the other books written by the same author, Sammy Hermans, such as: "How to control your kids with Yoga?", "The Yoga body book", "Happy Yoga", "Loving pregnancy thanks to Yoga" "99 Reasons to do Yoga" and more coming.

Every time that you buy a book from the author, you are supporting the author to do more research and write more books that can help you in different ways. Every book can give you more insights to Yoga and can help you for a more healthy and happier life.

If you have any suggestions or comments, you can report them any time by filling in the contact form at the website www.yogalatinos.com.

Please support

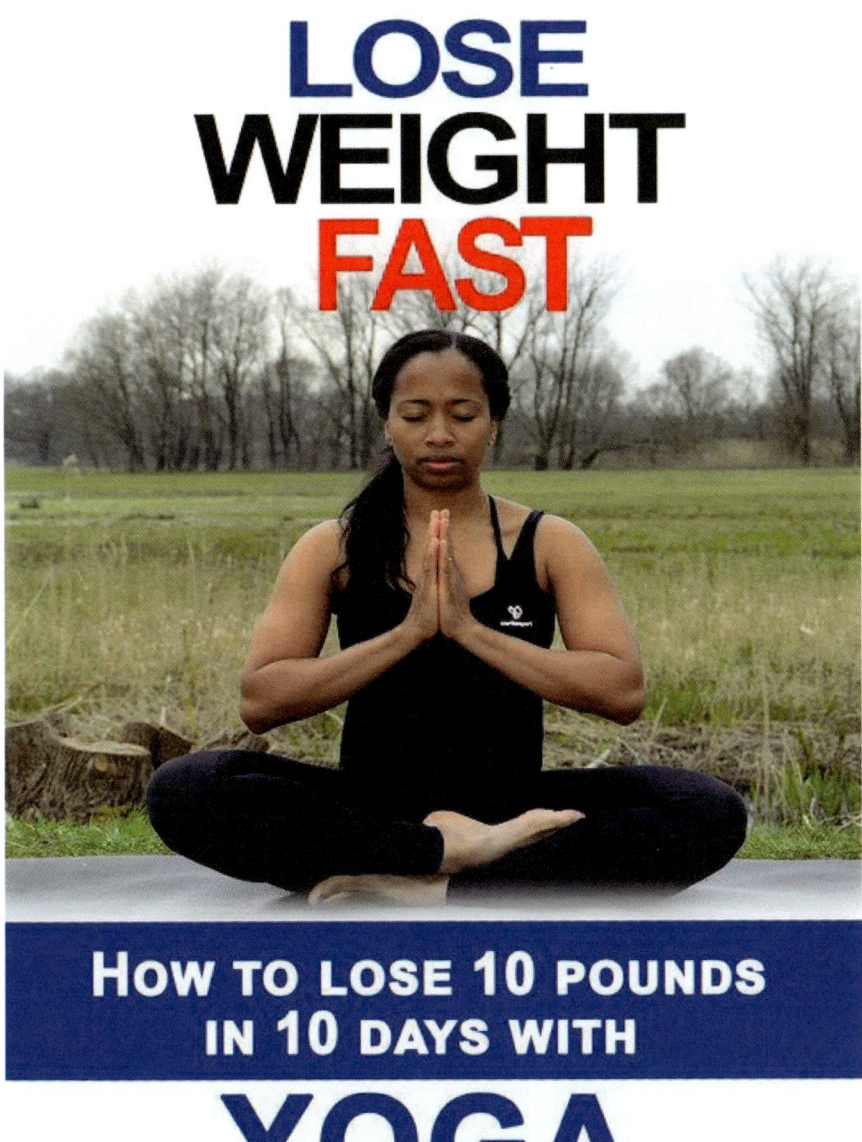

Thanks a lot for the support!

Extra Bonus

Chapter 1: Can the 10 DAYS program really work for me?

Many people believe that weight loss arises from excessively strict dieting, strenuous cardio and even weight training; Yoga may frequently be overlooked as an option for weight loss as it is not commonly thought of as a slimming exercise.

However, Yoga should be considered for weight loss as there are many benefits to participating in this exercise. Yoga allows for participants to strengthen their inner core muscles and build strength. Whilst this form of exercise may not burn an extensive amount of calories, it allows for the individual to train their mind to make healthier choices.

This new way of healthier thinking promotes healthy choices relating to the individual's body, such as the decision to eat healthier foods and participate in more regular physical activity.

Whilst Yoga traditionally does not burn the calories that walking or running does, Yoga helps a person increase their own mindfulness, particularly how they think of and relate to their own self and body.

For example, regular participation in Yoga allows one to develop a deep sense of understanding about their body, and even a connection with themselves and their health. An avid Yoga participant will be aware of how they are feeling internally, and additionally will understand what foods make their body feel better or worse.

This will help to promote healthier choices in relation to the consumption of certain foods; therefore, Yoga, through promoting an awareness of self, promotes healthy eating choices and therefore weight loss.

A common question posed by many who are unfamiliar with Yoga and the related benefits is often "can Yoga really work for me?" The answer is simple: **YES!** Yoga can work for anyone who is open to participating in an activity that will allow the person to relate to and connect with their body. "Can this 10 days Yoga food and Yoga exercise program work for me?" The answer is **YES!**

Here's why: primarily, Yoga involves continuous use of your muscles, which burns calories. This means that your muscles are continuously stretching and working, which means you are exercising, which in turn promotes weight loss. So, as a result, this aspect of participating in the activity alone means Yoga will work for you as a form of weight loss!

Furthermore, this program only requires 15 minutes of Yoga exercise per day, so it's easy to participate and get motivated!

The second aspect of this 10 days program is the food. Following this diet that has been provided to you will not only decrease your calorie intake to a healthier level, but will also promote an increase in your metabolism, thus enhancing weight loss. Weight loss typically occurs when a person's calorie intake is less than their calorie expenditure. Simply put, if you burn more calories than you eat, your body will be forced to burn its own fat storage, causing you to lose weight.

The foods chosen in this 10 days Yoga food and Yoga exercise program are designed to work in combination with a Yoga exercise program to maximize your weight loss! The particular foods have been proven to satisfy hunger and cravings even though they are low in calories; the perfect combination for weight loss!

Furthermore, the food chosen for this Yoga food and Yoga exercise program are portioned in realistic sizes, unlike many other diets that leave you feeling hungry. After reading the book you should be able to learn more about your own body and feel when to stop eating; in order to avoid eating too many calories.

This program considers the individual; foods have been chosen that are tasty and won't make you feel like you're on a 10 days diet. Most people may even continue the food plan after the 10 days because it is a realistic way that is not a diet, but a lifestyle and a way of eating healthier. The results speak for themselves and you will see these results yourself after your 10 days participation!

In conclusion, will this program work for you? The answer is, **Yes.** This 10 days Yoga food and Yoga exercise program will have you connect with your inner self and make healthier choices that promote weight loss. This program will promote daily exercise to tone and tighten your body in combination with a diet that will speed up your metabolism and burn fat.

The program will work for you because even from day 1 you will feel as though you are not on a diet or completing a rigorous exercise scheme, but rather you are making a life change to improve your overall health and well being; what could possible feel better than that?

Start Yoga Today!

Printed in Poland
by Amazon Fulfillment
Poland Sp. z o.o., Wrocław